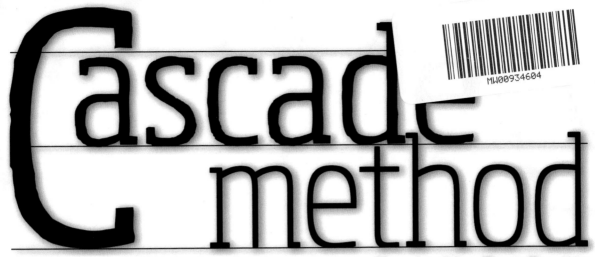

Cascade method

Created by Tara Boykin

This book belongs to

Chords 1

INDEX

BONUS SNOWMAN PAGES!

C Major Chords

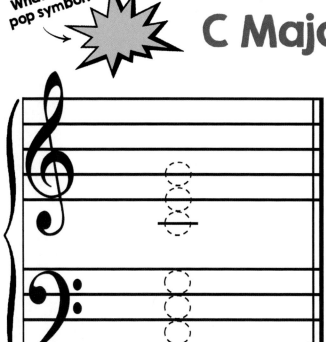

Trace the C major chords in the treble clef and bass clef!

and

Color in the corresponding C major chords on NoteMatch!

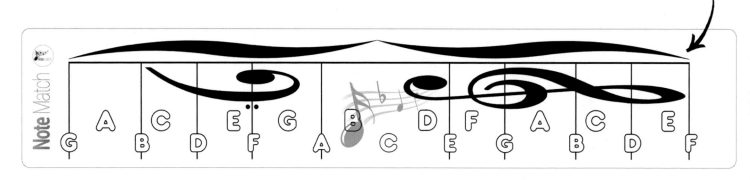

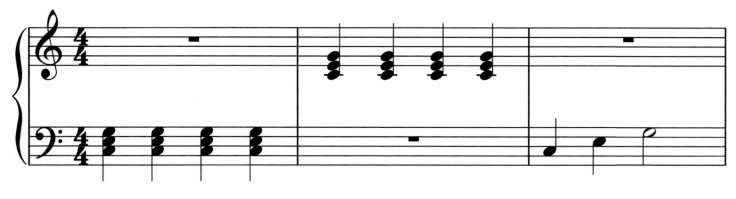

4

Play Composer!

It's time to 'play composer' and write your own piece in C major!

All of the faint notes below are C, E and G's which all belong to a C major chord.

You can trace up to 3 notes in either or both of the treble clef or the bass clef.

Write your name here! You are the composer!

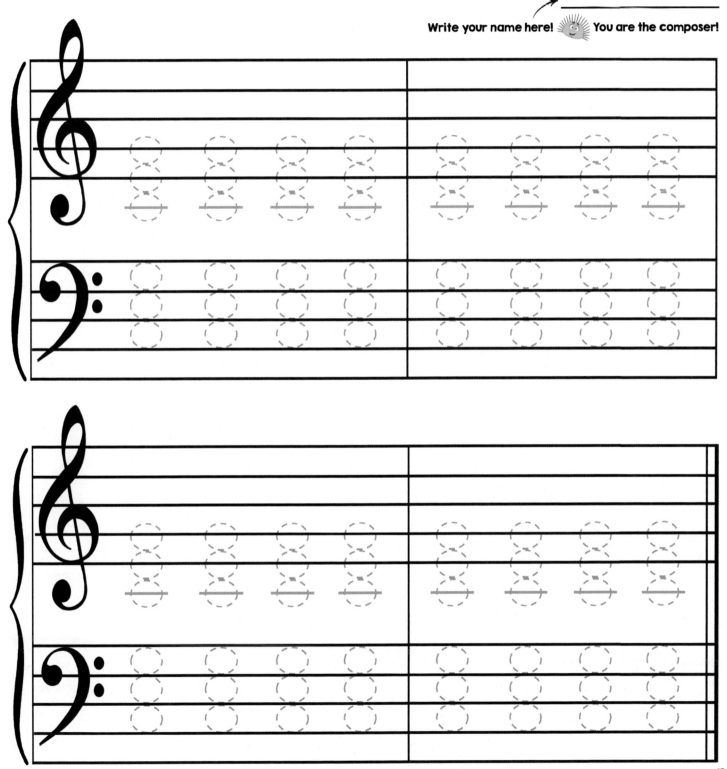

5

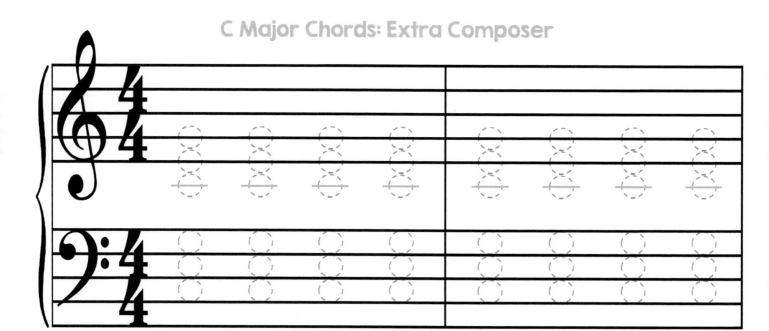

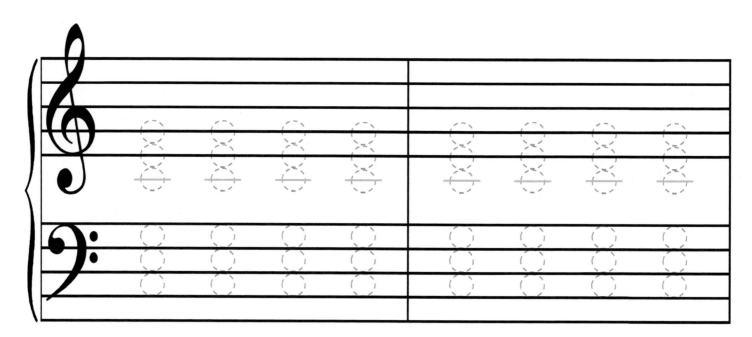

Happy to  You!

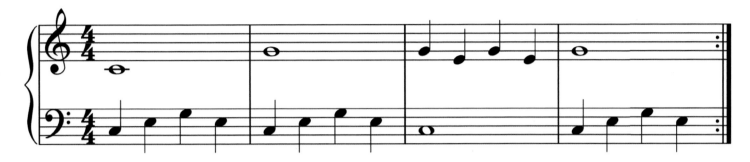

 Tip: Find the 9 imposter notes! Color, highlight or circle them.
Name those imposters: R.H. _____ & _____

C Minor Chords

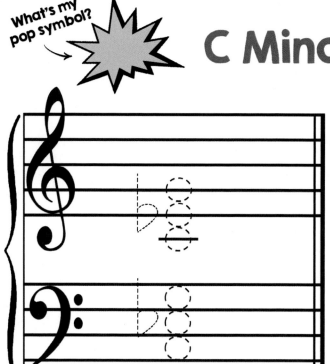

Trace the C minor chords in the treble clef and bass clef!

and

Color in the corresponding C minor chords and trace the flat signs on NoteMatch!

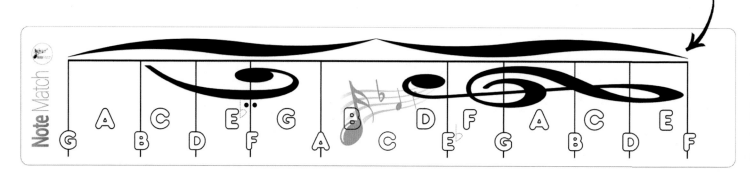

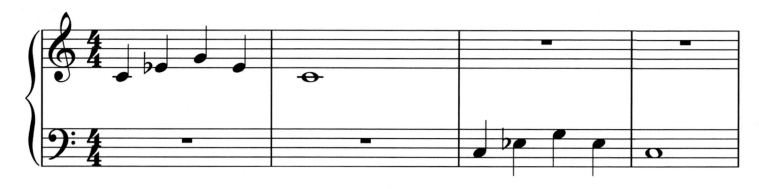

Play Composer!

It's time to 'play composer' and write your own piece in C minor!

All of the faint notes below are C, E♭ and G's which all belong to a C minor chord.

You can trace up to 3 notes in either or both of the treble clef or the bass clef.

 The flat rule: The first E you choose to add a flat in front of will make ALL the following E's flat, in that measure. Use this rule for every measure!

Write your name here! _____ You are the composer!

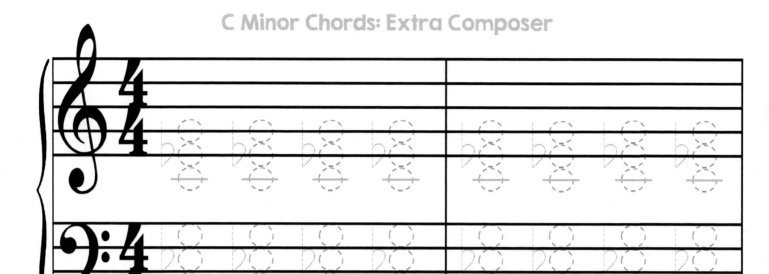

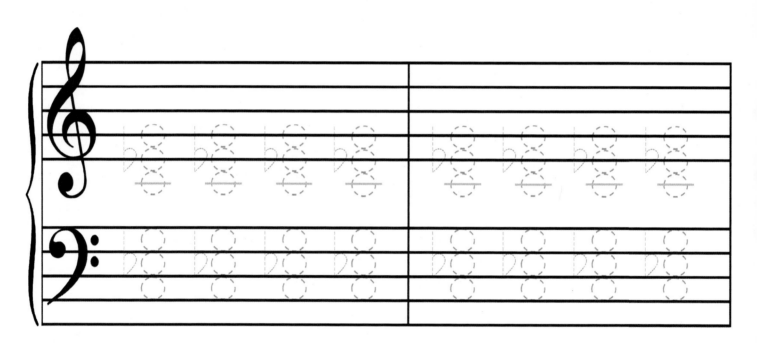

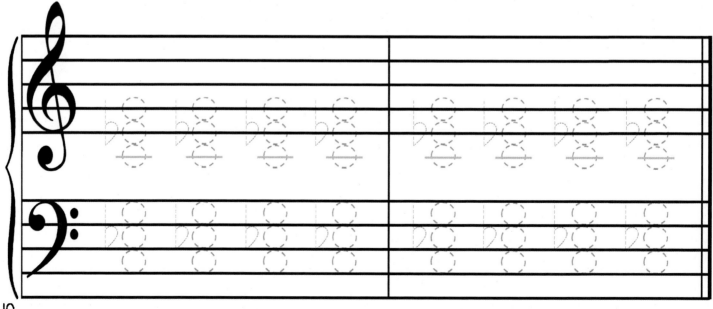

Sneaky Hunter

D Major Chords

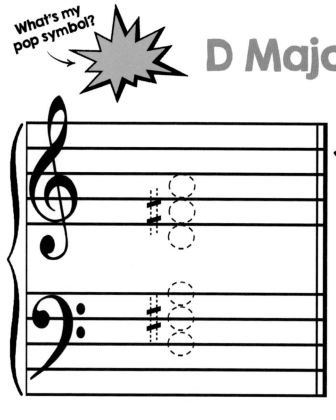

Trace the D major chords in the treble clef and bass clef!

and

Color in the corresponding D major chords and trace the sharps on NoteMatch!

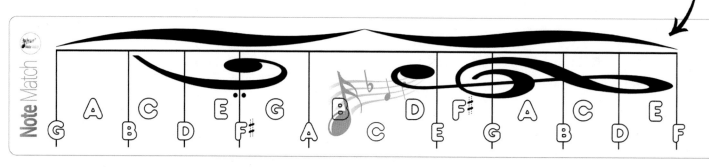

Play Composer!

It's time to 'play composer' and write your own piece in D major!

All of the faint notes below are D, F# and A's which all belong to a D major chord.

You can trace up to 3 notes in either or both of the treble clef or the bass clef.

 The sharp rule: The first F you choose to add a sharp in front of will make ALL the following F's sharp, in that measure. Use this rule for every measure!

Write your name here! You are the composer!

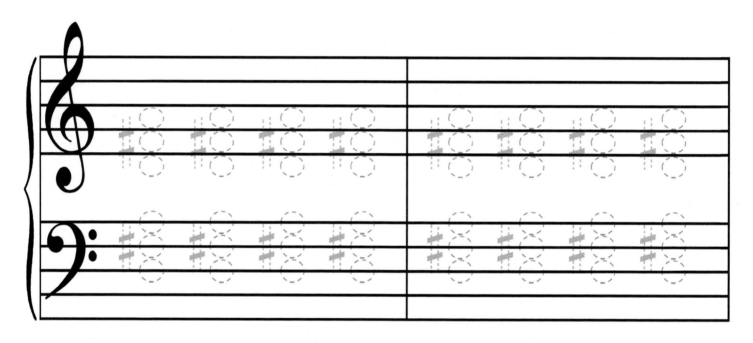

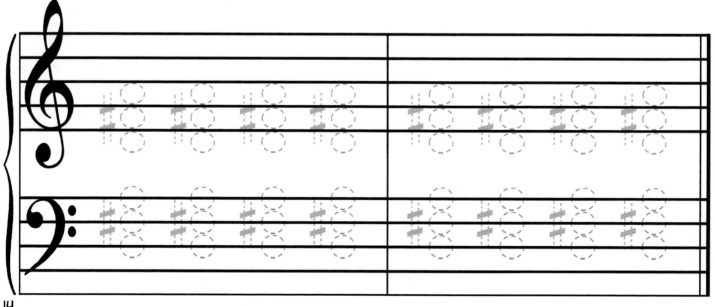

A Sunny Day

 Tip: Find the 11 imposter notes! Color, highlight or circle them.

Name those imposters: R.H. _____ & _____   L.H. _____ (this is a tricky one!)

15

D Minor Chords

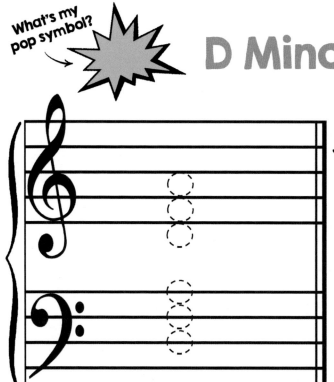

Trace the D minor chords in the treble clef and bass clef!

and

Color in the corresponding D minor chords on NoteMatch!

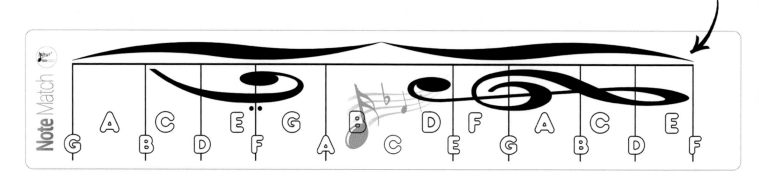

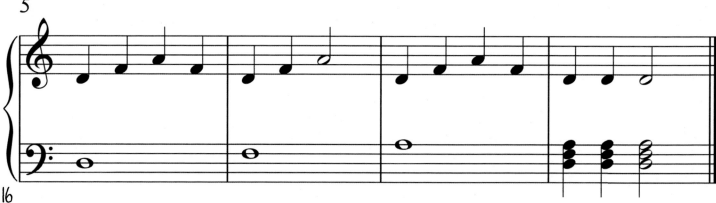

Play Composer!

It's time to 'play composer' and write your own piece in D minor!

All of the faint notes below are D, F and A's which all belong to a D minor chord.

You can trace up to 3 notes in either or both of the treble clef or the bass clef.

Write your name here! You are the composer!

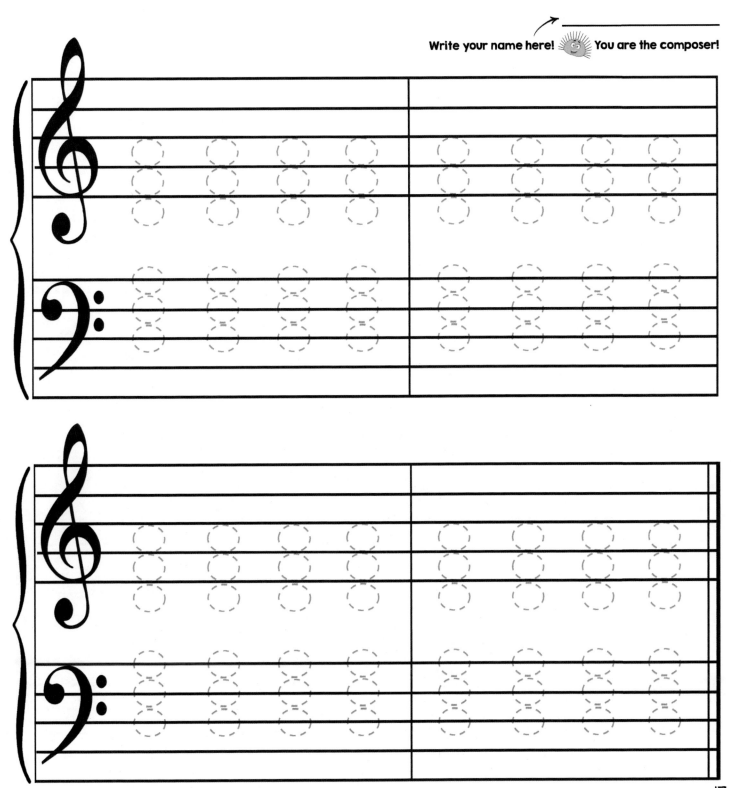

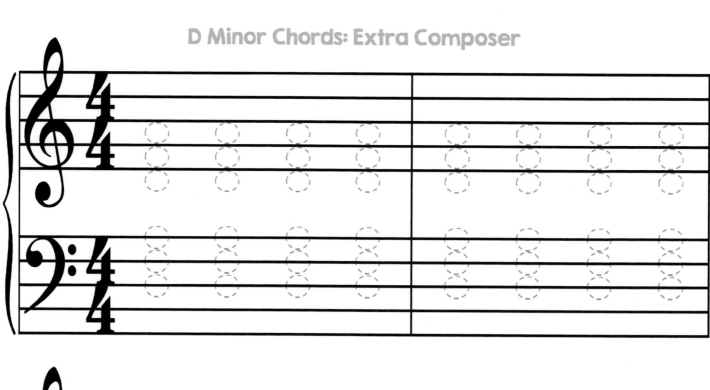

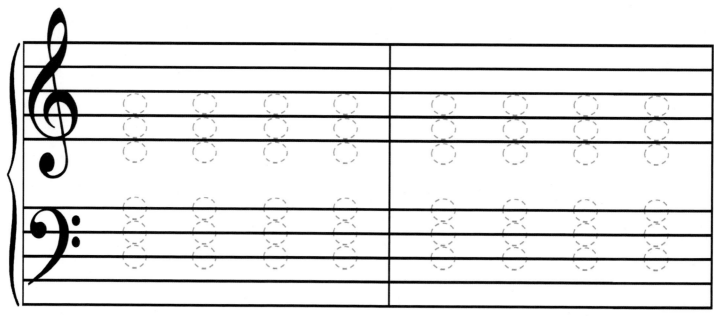

The Playful Horse

 Tip: Find the 10 imposter notes! Color, highlight or circle them.
Name those imposters: R.H. _____ & _____ **L.H.** _____

E Major Chords

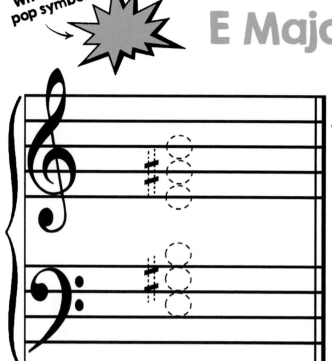

Trace the E major chords in the treble clef and bass clef!

and

Color in the corresponding E major chords and trace the sharps on NoteMatch!

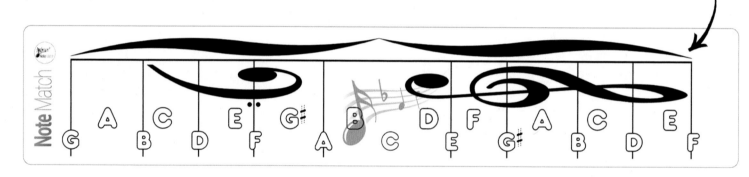

Play Composer!

It's time to 'play composer' and write your own piece in E major!

All of the faint notes below are E, G# and B's which all belong to an E major chord.

You can trace up to 3 notes in either or both of the treble clef or the bass clef.

⚠️ **The sharp rule:** The first G you choose to add a sharp in front of will make ALL the following G's sharp, in that measure. Use this rule for every measure!

Write your name here! 🌞 You are the composer!

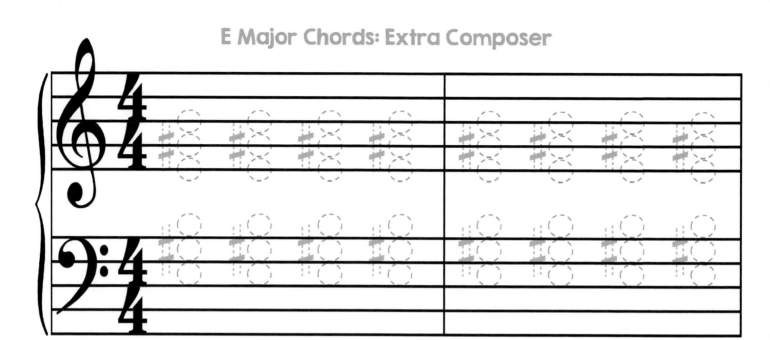

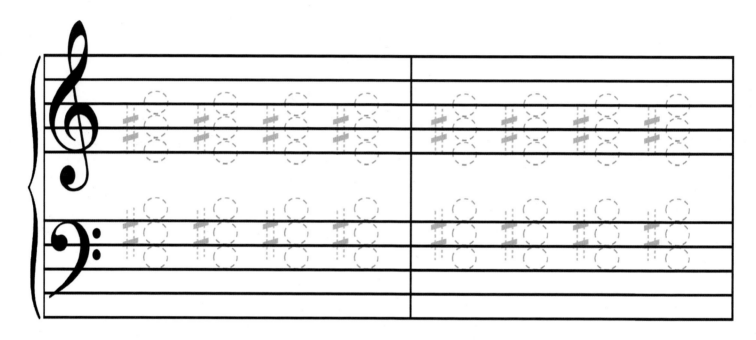

Chocolate Chip Cookies

 Tip: Find the 17 imposter notes! Color, highlight or circle them.
Name those imposters: R.H. _____ **&** _____   **L.H.** _____

23

E Minor Chords

What's my pop symbol?

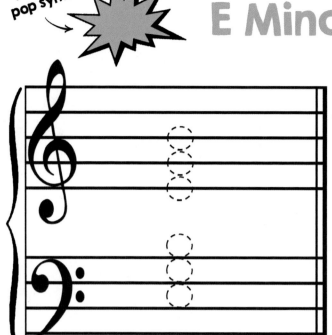

Trace the E minor chords in the treble clef and bass clef!

and

Color in the corresponding E minor chords on NoteMatch!

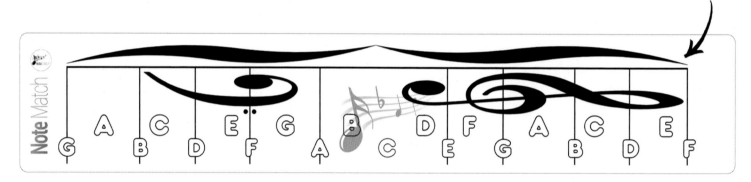

4

Play Composer!

It's time to 'play composer' and write your own piece in E minor!

All of the faint notes below are E, G and B's which all belong to an E minor chord.

You can trace up to 3 notes in either or both of the treble clef or the bass clef.

Write your name here! You are the composer!

25

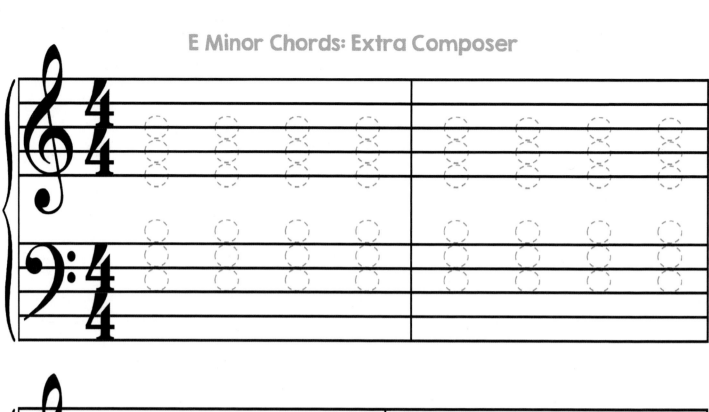

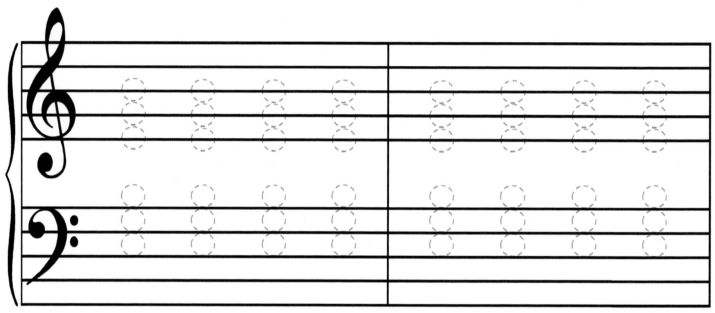

The Lonely Mime

Tip 1: Make a box around the C chord part and the 2 D chords parts.
Color the imposters within the boxes.

Tip 2: Color the 5 imposter notes anyhere outside of those boxes.

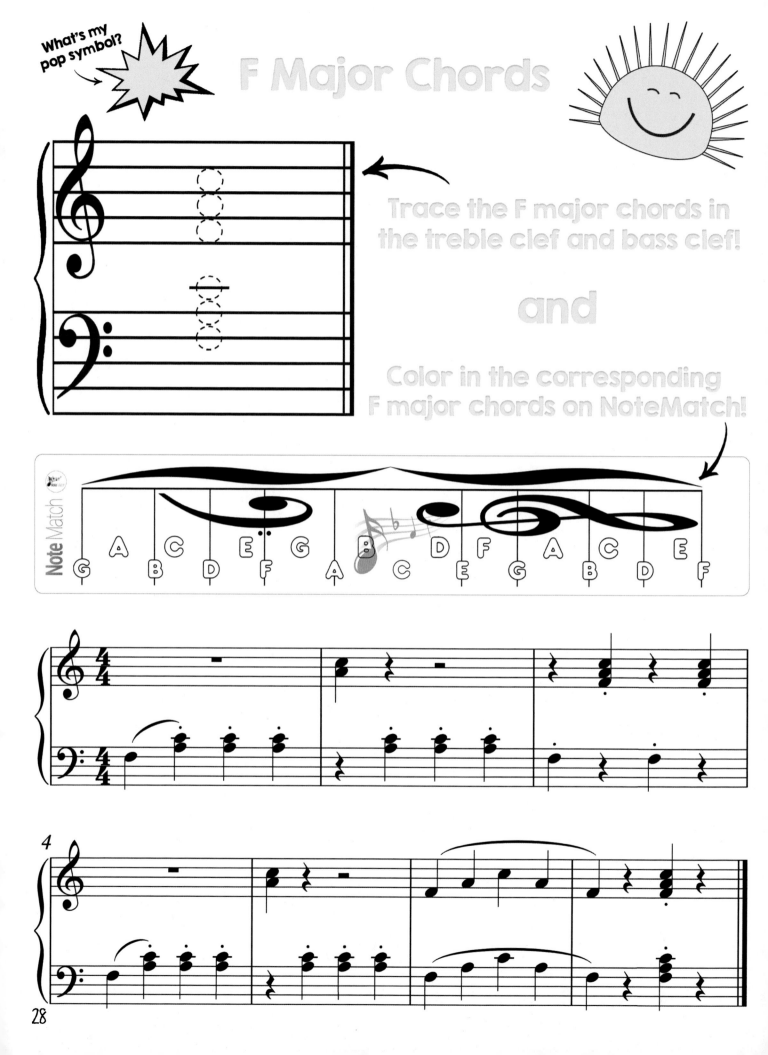

F Major Chords

What's my pop symbol?

Trace the F major chords in the treble clef and bass clef!

and

Color in the corresponding F major chords on NoteMatch!

Play Composer!

It's time to 'play composer' and write your own piece in F major!

All of the faint notes below are F, A and C's which all belong to an F major chord.

You can trace up to 3 notes in either or both of the treble clef or the bass clef.

Write your name here! You are the composer!

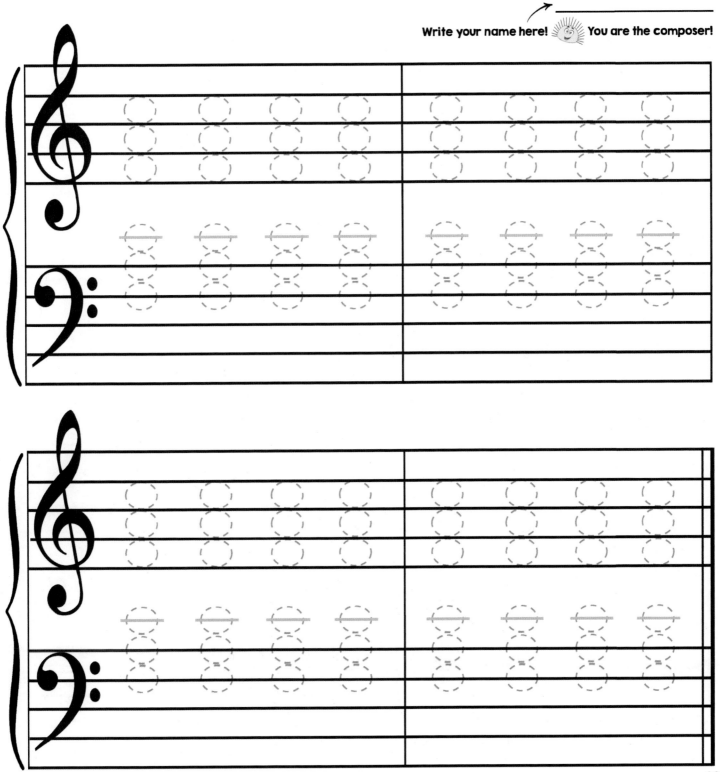

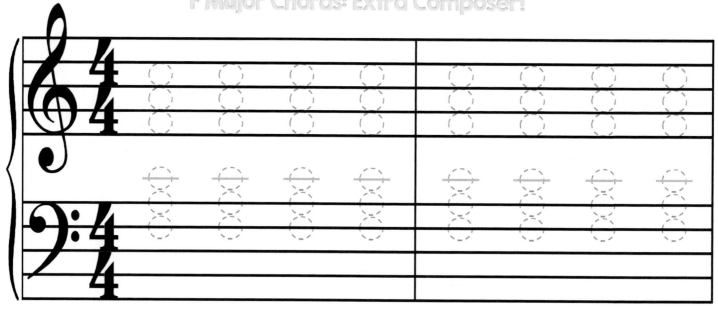

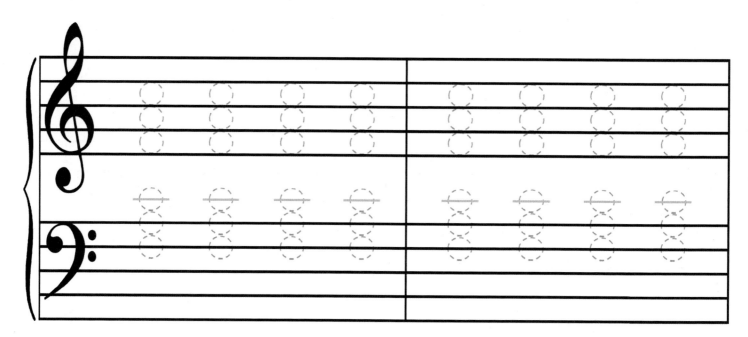

Funny Bunny

Tip 1: Make a box around the C chord part. Color the imposters within the box.

Tip 2: Color the 4 imposter notes in the rest of the piece.

Name those imposters: R.H. _____ & _____

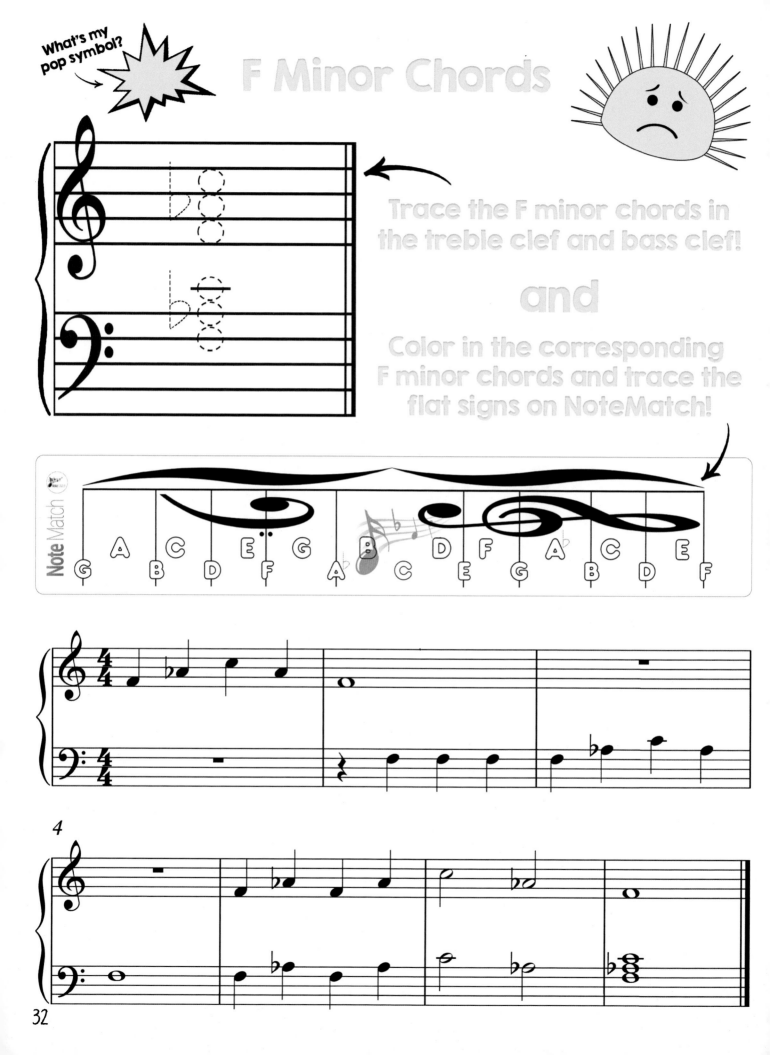

Play Composer!

It's time to 'play composer' and write your own piece in F major!

All of the faint notes below are F, A♭ and C's which all belong to an F major chord.

You can trace up to 3 notes in either or both of the treble clef or the bass clef.

 The flat rule: The first A you choose to add a flat in front of will make ALL the following A's flat, in that measure. Use this rule for every measure!

Write your name here! You are the composer!

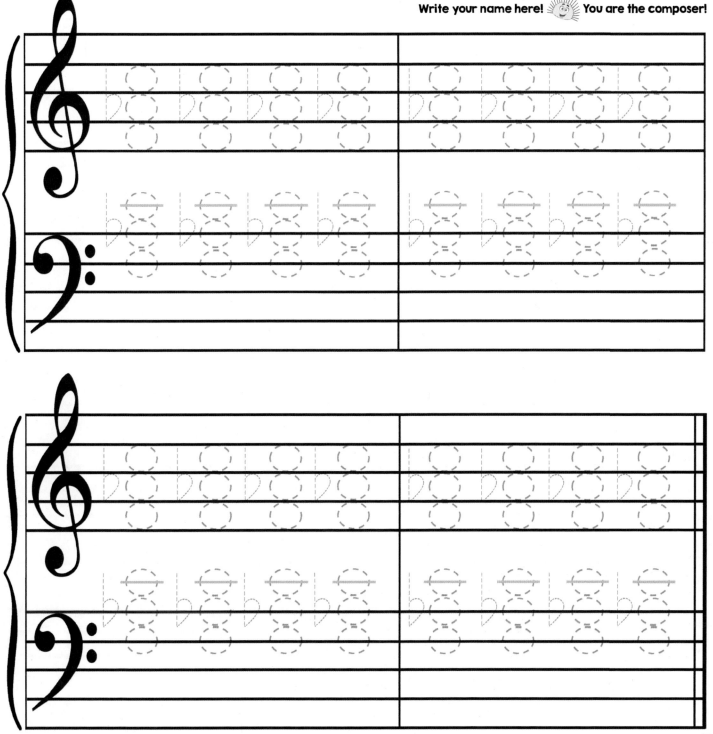

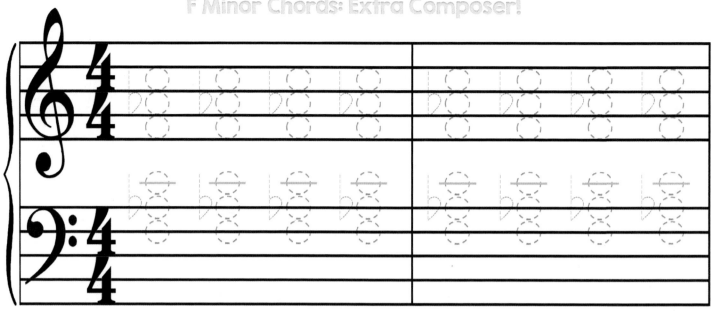

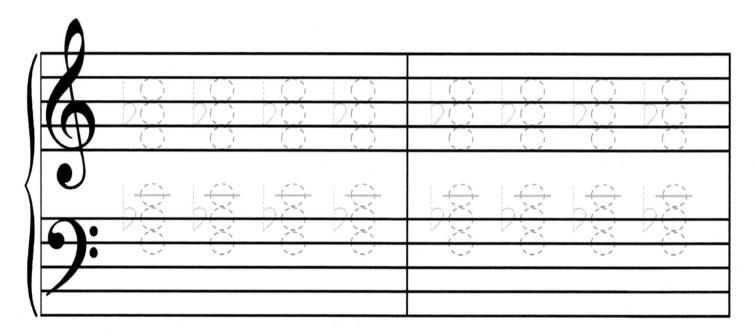

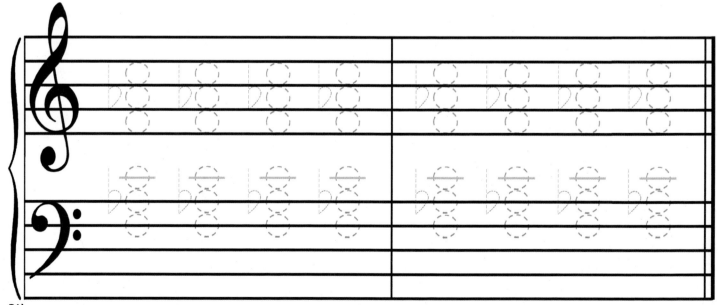

34

Rainy Days

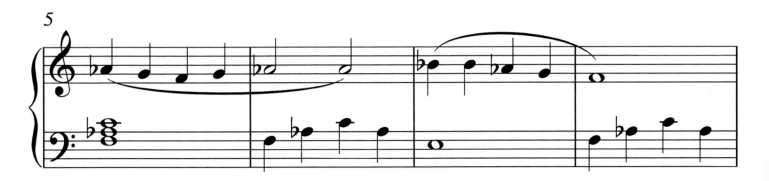

 Tip: Find the 24 imposter notes! Color, highlight or circle them.
Name those imposters: R.H. _____ & _____ L.H. _____

G Major Chords

Trace the G major chords in the treble clef and bass clef!

and

Color in the corresponding G major chords on NoteMatch!

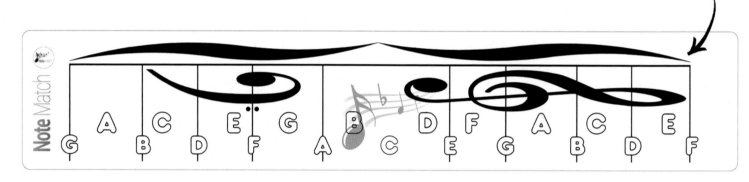

Play Composer!

It's time to 'play composer' and write your own piece in G major!

All of the faint notes below are G, B and D's which all belong to a G major chord.

You can trace up to 3 notes in either or both of the treble clef or the bass clef.

Write your name here! You are the composer!

37

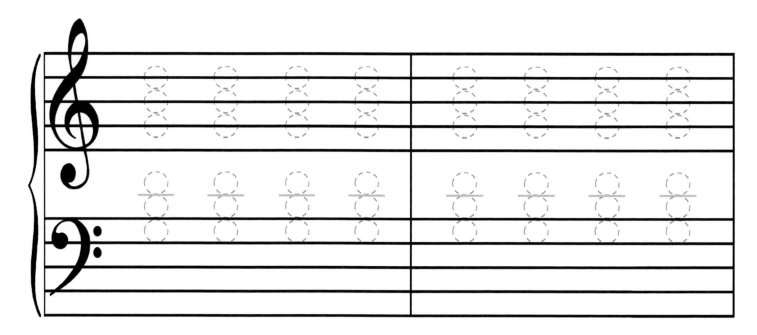

Happy Camper

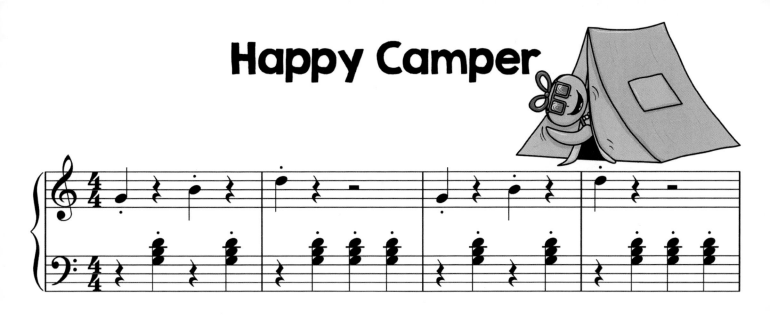

 Tip: Find the 6 imposter notes! Color, highlight or circle them.
Name those imposters: R.H. _____ L.H. _____

G Minor Chords

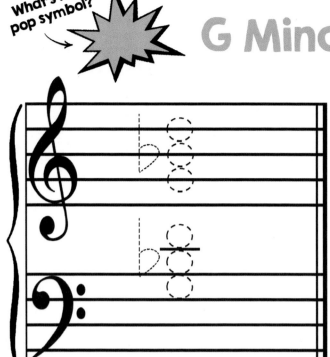

Trace the G minor chords in the treble clef and bass clef!

and

Color in the corresponding G minor chords and trace the flat signs on NoteMatch!

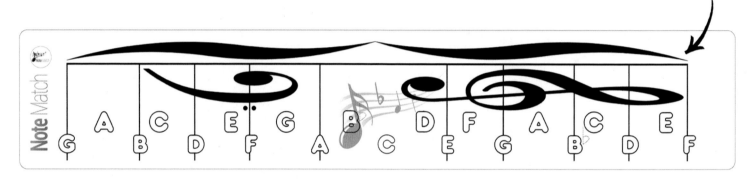

40

Play Composer!

It's time to 'play composer' and write your own piece in G minor!

All of the faint notes below are G, B♭ and D's which all belong to a G minor chord.

You can trace up to 3 notes in either or both of the treble clef or the bass clef.

 The flat rule: The first B you choose to add a flat in front of will make ALL the following B's flat, in that measure. Use this rule for every measure!

Write your name here! You are the composer!

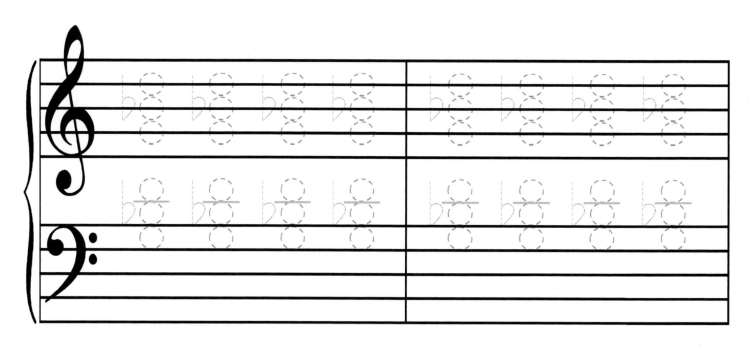

River Otter

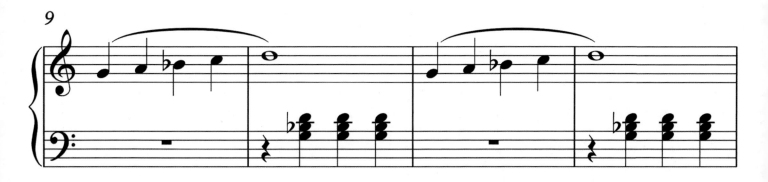

 Tip: Find the 20 imposter notes! Color, highlight or circle them.
Name those imposters: R.H. _____ & _____   L.H. _____ & _____

A Major Chords

Trace the A major chords in the treble clef and bass clef!

and

Color in the corresponding A major chords and trace the sharps on NoteMatch!

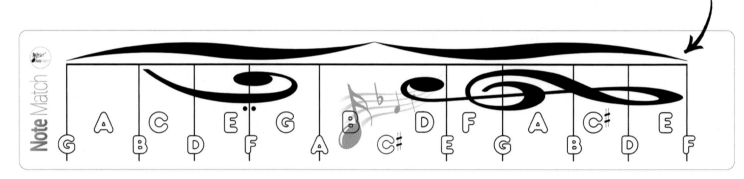

Play Composer!

It's time to 'play composer' and write your own piece in A major!

All of the faint notes below are A, C♯ and E's which all belong to an A major chord.

You can trace up to 3 notes in either or both of the treble clef or the bass clef.

 The sharp rule: The first C you choose to add a sharp in front of will make ALL the following C's sharp, in that measure. Use this rule for every measure!

Write your name here! You are the composer!

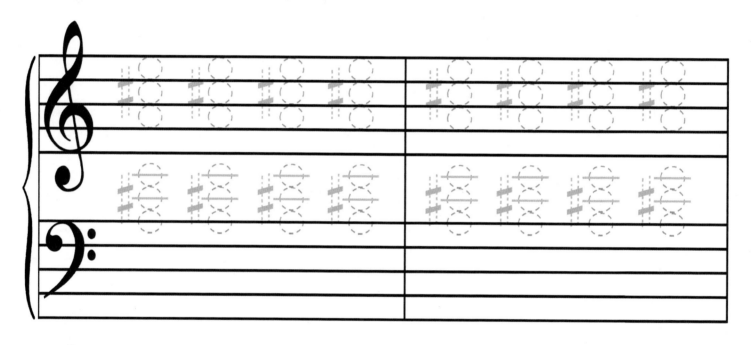

The Carousel

 Tip: Find the 11 imposter notes! Color, highlight or circle them.

Name those imposters: R.H. _____ & _____   L.H. _____ & _____

A Major Chords

What's my pop symbol?

These chords are getting mighty high! Let's try them an octave lower on NoteMatch!

Trace the low A major chords in the treble clef and bass clef. Color in the corresponding A major chords and trace the sharps on NoteMatch!

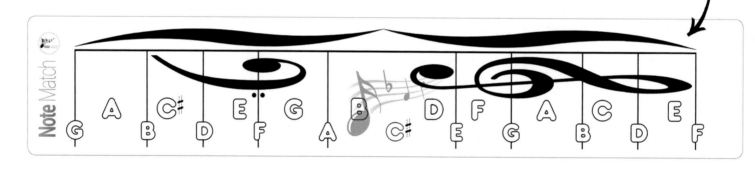

5

48

Play Composer!

It's time to 'play composer' and write your own piece in A major!

All of the faint notes below are A, C# and E's which all belong to an A major chord.

You can trace up to 3 notes in either or both of the treble clef or the bass clef.

 The sharp rule: The first C you choose to add a sharp in front of will make ALL the following C's sharp, in that measure. Use this rule for every measure!

Write your name here! You are the composer!

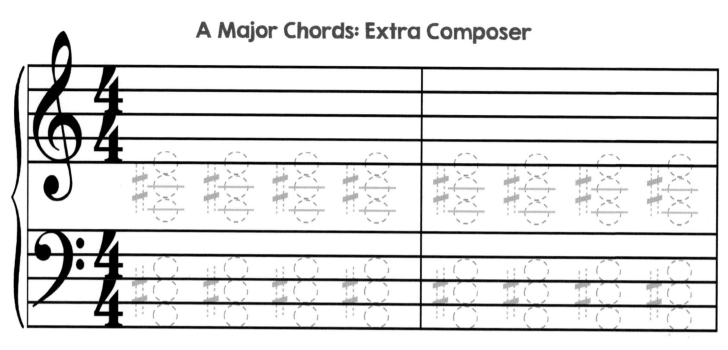

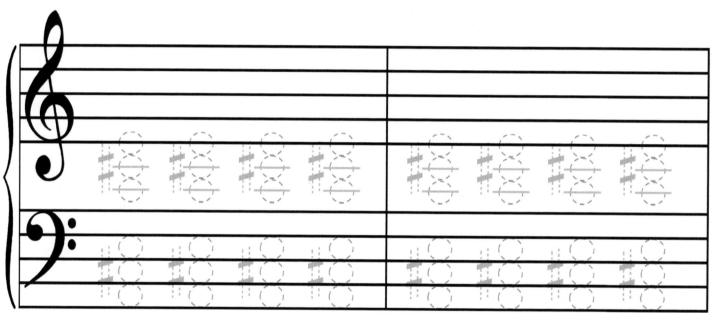

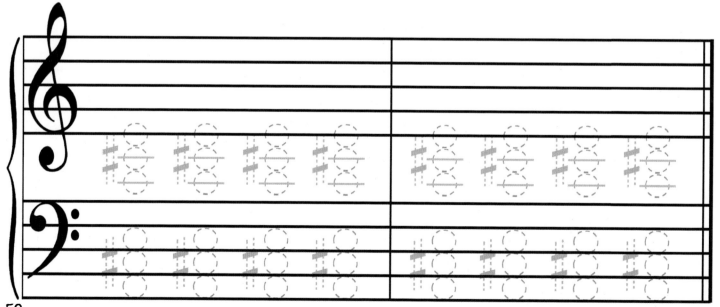

Campfire Dance

Tip: Find the 14 imposter notes! Color, highlight or circle them.

Name those imposters: R.H. ____ & ____   L.H. ____ & ____

A Minor Chords

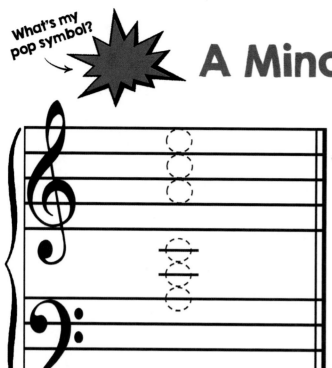

Trace the A minor chords in the treble clef and bass clef!

and

Color in the corresponding A minor chords on NoteMatch!

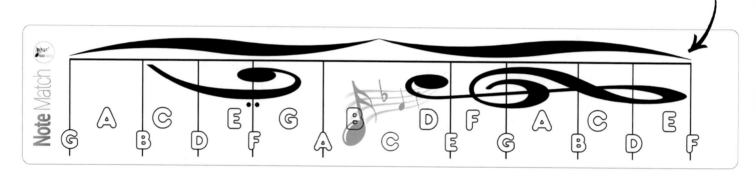

5

52

Play Composer!

It's time to 'play composer' and write your own piece in C minor!

All of the faint notes below are A, C and E's which all belong to an A minor chord.

You can trace up to 3 notes in either or both of the treble clef or the bass clef.

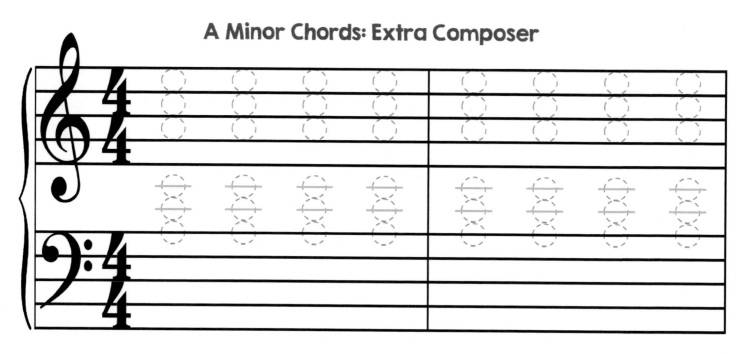

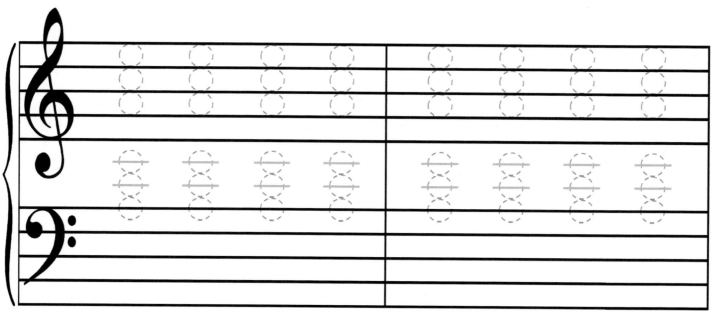

Sweet Lullaby

 Tip 1: Make a box around the two G chord parts. Color the imposters within the boxes.

Tip 2: Find the 3 imposter notes in the rest of the piece. Color, highlight or circle them.

A Minor Chords

These chords are getting mighty high! Let's try them an octave lower on NoteMatch!

Trace the lower A minor chords in the treble clef and bass clef, and color in the corresponding low A minor chords on NoteMatch!

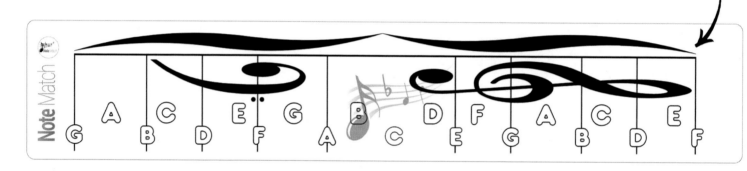

5

56

Play Composer!

It's time to 'play composer' and write your own piece in A minor!

All of the faint notes below are A, C and E's which all belong to an A minor chord.

You can trace up to 3 notes in either or both of the treble clef or the bass clef.

Write your name here! You are the composer!

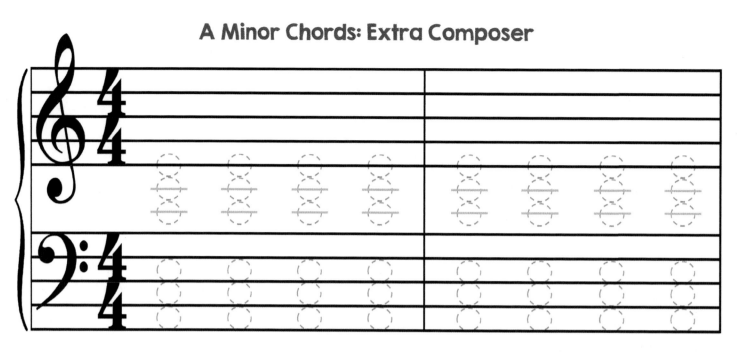

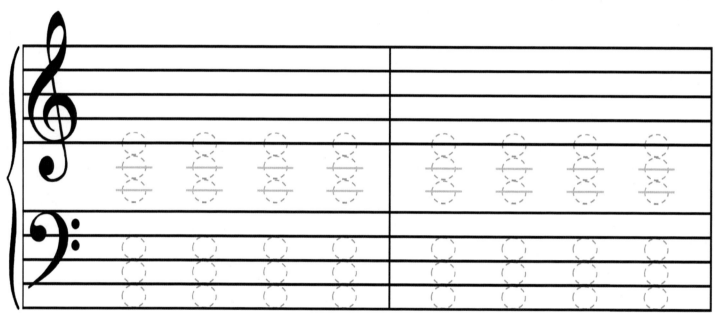

The Adventurous Ant

 Tip: Find the 17 imposter notes! Color, highlight or circle them.
Name the 3 different imposters: R.H. _____ & _____ LH: _____

B Major Chords

Trace the B major chords in the treble clef and bass clef!

and

Color in the corresponding B major chords and trace the sharps on NoteMatch!

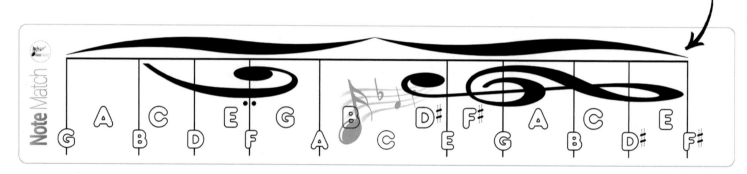

5

Play Composer!

It's time to 'play composer' and write your own piece in B major!

All of the faint notes below are B, D♯ and F♯'s which all belong to an B major chord.

You can trace up to 3 notes in either or both of the treble clef or the bass clef.

 The sharp rule: The first D and F you choose to add a sharp in front of will make ALL the following D's and F's sharp, in that measure. Use this rule for every measure!

Write your name here! You are the composer!

B Major Chords: Extra Composer

Little Ballerina

 Tip: Find the 12 imposter notes! Color, highlight or circle them.
Name those imposters: R.H. _____ & _____ L.H. _____

B Major Chords

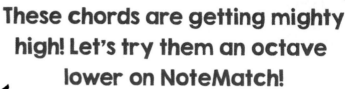

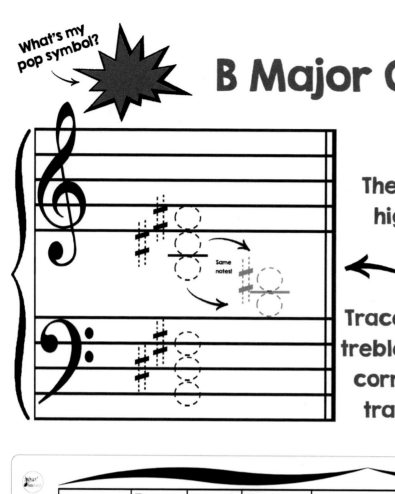

These chords are getting mighty high! Let's try them an octave lower on NoteMatch!

Trace the low B major chords in the treble clef and bass clef. Color in the corresponding B major chords and trace the sharps on MoteMatch!

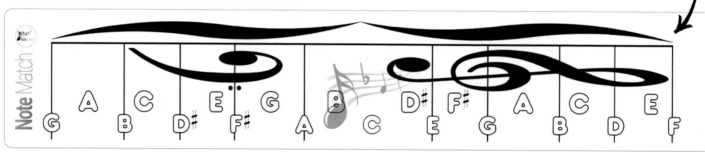

5

Play Composer!

It's time to 'play composer' and write a lower piece in B major!

All of the faint notes below are B, D# and F#'s which all belong to an B major chord.

You can trace up to 3 notes in either or both of the treble clef or the bass clef.

 The sharp rule: The first D and F you choose to add a sharp in front of will make ALL the following D's and F's sharp, in that measure. Use this rule for every measure!

Write your name here! You are the composer!

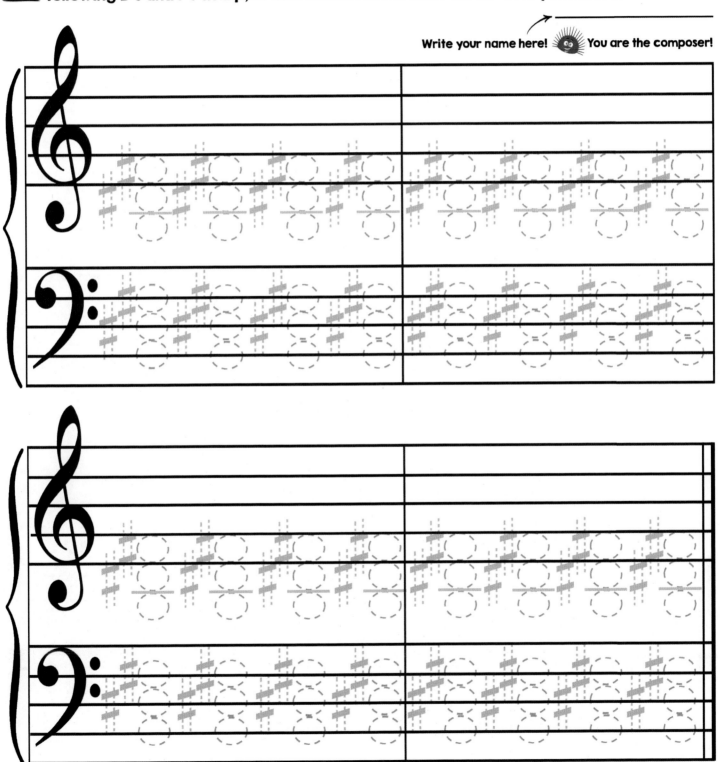

B Major Chords: Extra Composer

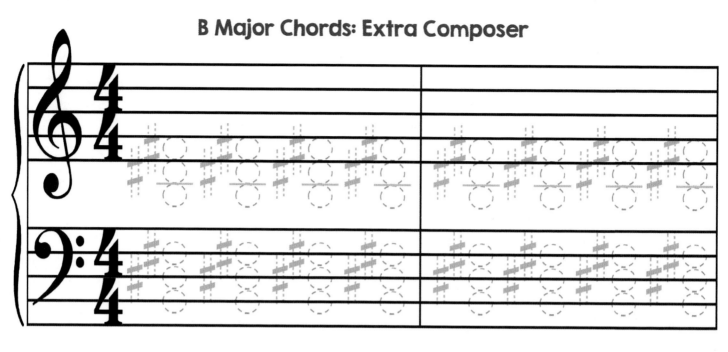

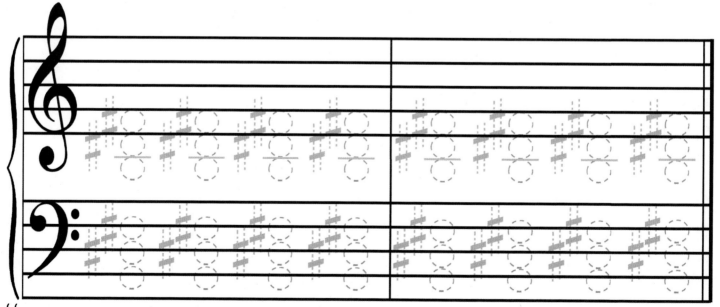

The Juggler

 Tip 1: Make a box around the E chord measure.

Tip 2: Find the 3 imposter notes in the rest of the piece!
Color, highlight or circle them. Name that imposter: R.H. _____

67

B Minor Chords

What's my pop symbol?

Same notes!

Trace the B minor chords in the treble clef and bass clef!

and

Color in the corresponding B minor chords and trace the sharp signs on NoteMatch!

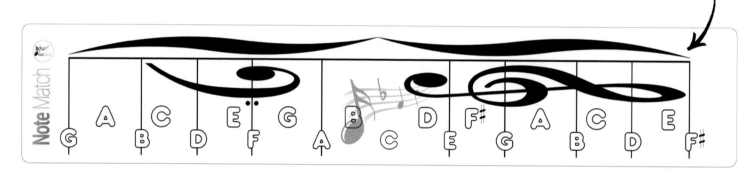

Play Composer!

It's time to 'play composer' and write your own piece in B minor!

All of the faint notes below are B, D and F#'s which all belong to an B minor chord.

You can trace up to 3 notes in either or both of the treble clef or the bass clef.

 The sharp rule: The first F you choose to add a sharp in front of will make ALL the following F's sharp, in that measure. Use this rule for every measure!

Write your name here! _____ You are the composer!

Dreaming of YESTERDAY

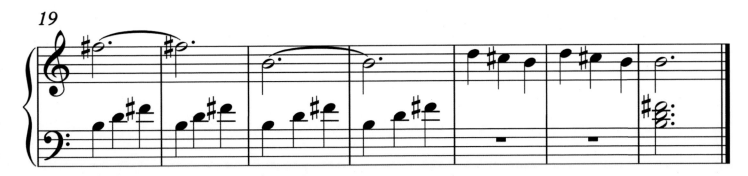

Tip 1: Make a big box around line 2. Write in the 3 L.H. notes.

Tip 2: Make a big box around line 2. Name the L.H. chord and color the imposters!

Tip 3: Find the 4 imposter notes from line 1 and 4! Color, highlight or circle them.
Name that one imposter note: R.H. _____

B Minor Chords

What's my pop symbol?

Same notes!

These chords are getting mighty high! Let's try them an octave lower on NoteMatch!

Trace the lower B minor chords in the treble clef and bass clef. Color in the corresponding low B minor chords and trace the sharp signs on NoteMatch!

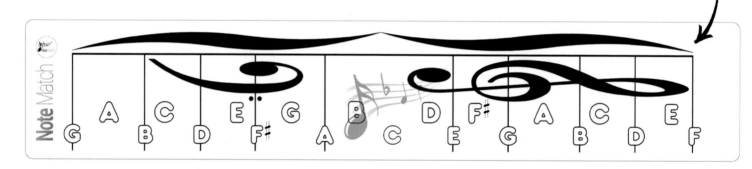

Play Composer!

It's time to play composer and write a lower piece in B minor!

All of the faint notes below are B, D and F#'s which all belong to an B minor chord.

You can trace up to 3 notes in either or both of the treble clef or the bass clef.

⚠️ The sharp rule: The first F you choose to add a sharp in front of will make ALL the following F's sharp, in that measure. Use this rule for every measure!

Write your name here! 😊 You are the composer!

73

B MinorChords: Extra Composer

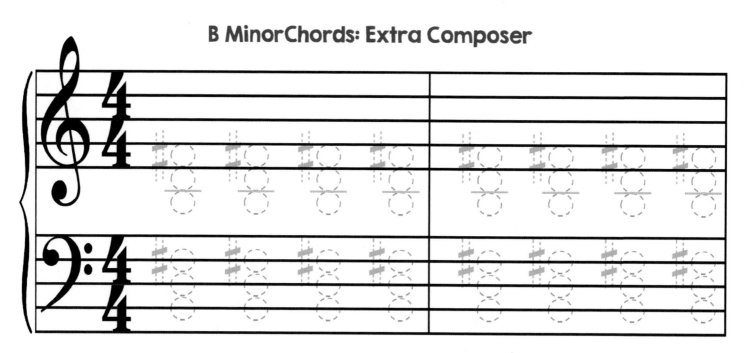

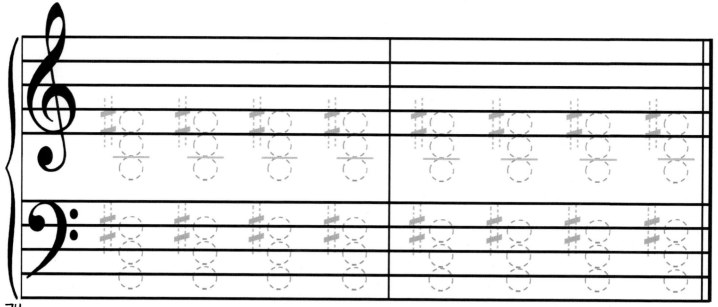

Soldier March

Tip 1: Make a box around the A chord part.

**Tip 2: Find the 10 imposter notes in the rest of the piece! Color, highlight or circle
them. Name those imposters: R.H. _____ , _____ & _____   L.H. _____**

Major Chords

Chords are SO easy to identify because they look like a snowman! Once you notice a "snowman" in your piano piece, all you need to do is figure out the bottom note and the rest is easy to play!

directions:

1. In the snowman, write the note of the bottom snowball and give him a smile!

2. Play the chord! Tip 1: Look what clef the snowman is in! Tip 2: Use NoteMatch to find the bottom notes!

What are the 3 different "all white" major chords? _____ , _____ , and _____ !

Because all of the snowmen above are "happy" snowmen, you now know how to write the symbol of a Major Chord! All you need is a CAPITAL LETTER! Not only are you a pro at finding AND playing chords, you know how to write pop symbols for major chords! High five!

Minor Chords

diRections:

1. In the snowman, write the note of the bottom snowball and give him a frown.

2. Write a lower case "m" next to the bottom snowball.

3. Play the chord! Tip 1: Look what clef the snowman is in! Tip 2: Use NoteMatch to find the bottom notes!

What are the 3 different "all white" minor chords? _____, _____, and _____!

All the snowmen above are "sad" snowmen because of their frowny face and the lower case "m" you put next to the letter in the bottom snowball. All you need is a CAPITAL LETTER + an "m" to write the pop symbol of a MINOR CHORD! You're now a minor chord pop symbol pro! WOOHOO!

Mix n' Match Major & Minor Chords

directions:

1. In the snowman, write the note of the bottom snowball.

2. Play the chord! Use your ear to figure out if it's a major or a minor chord.

If it sounds happy (major), add a smile, and if it sounds sad (minor), add a frown!

3. Write a lower case "m" next to the bottom snowball of all the sad snowmen.

78

Tricky Major Chords

Let's try the tricky major chords, the ones that have a sharp as a middle note. You can always start by playing the three white notes, and then adjust the middle note by going up to the VERY NEXT BLACK KEY.

directions:

1. In the snowman, write the note of the bottom snowball and then give him a smile!

2. Play the chord! Tip 1: Look what clef the snowman is in! Tip 2: Watch out for those sharps! Some may have 2!

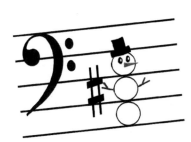

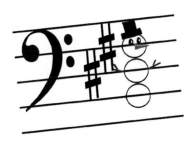

What are the 4 tricky major chords? _____, _____, _____, and _____!

Tricky Minor Chords

Let's try the tricky minor chords, the ones that have a sharp or a flat as a middle note. You can always start by playing the three white notes, and then adjust the middle note by going up or down to the VERY NEXT BLACK KEY.

diRections:

1. In the snowman, write the note of the bottom snowball and then give him a frown!

2. Write a lower case "m" next to the bottom snowball.

3. Play the chord! Tip 1: Look what clef the snowman is in! Tip 2: Watch out for those sharps and flats!

What are the 3 tricky minor chords? _____, _____, and _____!

Mix n' Match Tricky Major & Minor Chords

diRections:

1. In the snowman, write the note of the bottom snowball.

2. Play the chord! Watch out for sharps and flats! Use your ear to figure out if it's a major or a minor chord. Add a smile to the major chords, and a frown to the minor chords.

3. Write a lower case "m" next to the bottom snowball of all the sad snowmen.

Major Chord Pop Symbols

Let's try this the other way around, where the pop symbol is already written in! All the snowmen below are happy so they already have a smile on their face!

diRections:

1. **Look at the pop symbol in the snowman's bottom snowball, then play the chord.**

2. **Add a sharp to the middle note if the chord sounds sad. If it sounds happy, no need to do anything!** Tip 1: Look what clef the snowman is in! Tip 2: B major chords need a sharp for the top note too!

Minor Chord Pop Symbols

Let's try this the other way around, where the pop symbol is already written in! All the snowmen below are sad so they already have a frown on their face!

directions:

1. Look at the pop symbol in the snowman's **bottom** snowball, then play the chord.

2. Add a flat to the middle note if the chord sounds happy. If it sounds sad, no need to do anything! Tip 1: Look what clef the snowman is in! Tip 2: B minor chords need a sharp for the top note!

Mix n' Match Pop Symbols

It's time to mix n' match these major and minor pop symbols! We've mixed the happy and sad snowmen!

diRections:

1. Look at the pop symbol in the snowman's bottom snowball, then play the chord.

2. Add a sharp or a flat to the middle note according to the pop symbol. Use your ear!

Tip 1: Look what clef the snowman is in!　　Tip 2: Watch out for those tricky B chords! you know the drill!

Cascade Method Certificate

Congratulations
to

_____

for finishing the
Chords I
Book!

Teacher: _____ **Date:** _____

Made in the USA
Monee, IL
13 September 2022

13920198R00052